TO SAVE
CUT THE GOVERNING
STRUCTURES

TO SAVE CUT THE GOVERNING STRUCTURES

We are OVER Governed—
Here's a cutting guide

Carlton W. Laird

Copyright © 2011 by Carlton W. Laird.

Library of Congress Control Number:		2011904603
ISBN:	Hardcover	978-1-4568-9148-0
	Softcover	978-1-4568-9147-3
	Ebook	978-1-4568-9149-7

All rights reserved. No part of this book may be reproduced or transmitted in any form or by any means, electronic or mechanical, including photocopying, recording, or by any information storage and retrieval system, without permission in writing from the copyright owner.

This book was printed in the United States of America.

To order additional copies of this book, contact:
Xlibris Corporation
1-888-795-4274
www.Xlibris.com
Orders@Xlibris.com
96581

CONTENTS

The Public Voice Needs to be Heard 13
Transfer Most of Federal Government to States 15
Reduce the Size of the Federal Government 17
Why Cling to Custom and Tradition? 18
An Improved Government is Waiting 20
For Your Consideration 22
A Time Tested Solution 25
Problems Facing Philadelpia II 28
An Alternative to Congress 30
Cost Reduction Continued 32
Defining Real Wealth 34
Move State Legislatures Out of State Capitals 36
Changing Old Customs 38
Has Prohibition Ever Worked? 41
There is More Waste 44
Is There A Wake Up Call? 50
The Mother of All Rip-Offs 52
Fleecing the Public 57
A Bad Stumble 58
The Ghost of Old Europe 59
JFK Tried to Correct This System 61
Maintaining Freedom 63
In Summary 65

Other books by Carlton W. Laird

Never Vote For The Incumbent

Beware Of Talking Snakes

Direct Democracy

Oh The World Owes Us A Living

Re-Elect No One

An Autobiography

TO Millie

Repeating the same thing over and over and expect different results may be a sign of insanity. So to start something new it may save time if we review what has not worked for decades. Then ask a lot of questions like why do our elected Representatives—correct that to read our elected MISREPRESENTATIVE officials cut only programs providing Public services? Have you noticed those so-called Public Servants are not cutting the cost of supporting and maintaining Legislative and Administrative levels of Government? When you voted for those office holders did you really expect they would "represent you?" Do you think they might do so soon?

This book is about cutting out hundreds of billions of taxpayer dollars used to support our legislative and administrative groups in State and the federal Government where life style resembles Royalty. But we are in luck—one out of 50 States, Nebraska stands out; it demonstrated years ago that a unicameral form of Government reduces legislative costs by over 50%! Yes, Nebraska has had a unicameral State

Government for over 70 years and not once gave thought of returning to its former bicameral Government. So why do heavily taxed residents in 49 other States ignore these facts? Let's guess—until now the Public didn't seem to care what Government cost though the Public did grumble a lot!

If by chance the Public in the other 49 States are now thinking of cutting the cost of Government the credit for Nebraska's leadership belongs to the late Senator George Norris appointed by the Nebraska legislature to be their U. S. Senator in 1913. His appointment was only months before the 17th Amendment to our Constitution approved later in 1917 making U. S. Senators publicly elected. When the 1930s Depression occurred the Nation's economy was severely depressed and Senator Norris felt it a duty to help his State's taxpayers reduce the cost of their government. He traveled throughout Nebraska explaining a unicameral legislature and why it did not make sense to elect two different legislative bodies that eventually have to reconcile their differences through conferences, and all at great expense to the Nebraska residents. Senator Norris pointed out we are no longer pioneers, that we now have good media and communication systems to keep residents informed. Today Senator Norris's logic is further strengthened and improved with electronics that give instantaneous communications and yet 49 States still cling to CUSTOM & TRADITION handed down from our Pioneers more than two centuries ago. This neglect guaranteed the Public would continue to pay escalating cost of Government through loyalty to Party politics and assisted by voter lethargy. Blind loyalty to Party politics has evolved to its ultimate peak, namely, to DIVIDE AND CONQUER that results in stagnation and brings Government virtually to a standstill! Do Not Expect A Corrupted Political System To Correct Itself—the rot is thorough and like rotten apples or potatoes it must be thrown OUT!

Nebraskan's followed the advice of Senator Norris's and approved a unicameral State legislature in 1934. The number of State legislators was reduced from 133 to 49 saving Nebraska's taxpayers more than 50%, and these savings have continued year after year. That was 77 years ago and Nebraska voters have never considered returning to a bicameral form of legislature. Of course Nebraska had a Statesman in George Norris, something sorely lacking to date in other States!

Of course politicians resist such a change because their vested interests benefit from the status quo. A unicameral government removes the political objective to DIVIDE and CONTROL. Let's take a closer look at how Nebraska's unicameral system changed that.

THE PUBLIC VOICE NEEDS TO BE HEARD

Local candidates for Nebraska's State unicameral Senate can file for the office by Party affiliation if they choose but when elected they serve as a Non-partisan. Nebraska's residents provide the essential of a true democracy by assuming the role of CHECKS & BALANCE that our Founders believed necessary and so they created two houses, the Representatives and the Senate. The Pioneers did what was best for their widely scattered Pioneer population but why do we continue this for over 230 years when we have the media and electronic communications providing instant information? To further enhance Democracy through public participation Nebraska's Government provides several locations around the State where residents serve as the CHECKS AND BALANCE on pending legislative Bills. This is democracy in action that was not available to our Founders and their Pioneer constituents. In Nebraska the elected office is non-partisan so campaigns for office are oriented toward issues rather than continuing to divide people over Party loyalty that we all know makes no difference regardless of which Party is in power.

Today the Public in the other 49 States can choose (1) to keep what they have and pay escalating taxes for less and less services. Or (2) abandon the Pioneer's method of governing that still exists and prevents real democracy from working. Your tax bill could then be just a fraction of what you are now paying. Under plan (1) the Public's debt will keep increasing as legislators continue to issue more bonds to offset the shortfall in revenue. The interest on bonds simply adds to the debt that keeps increasing.

Relying on bonds to cover a revenue shortfall is an excuse for not assuming the cost we incur and with "indifference" we pass our debts to our heirs. It is a shallow, shameful attitude! Of course banks love government bonds for they collect interest annually on our debts. At the top of our Nation's banking syndicate is the Federal Reserve a privately owned collection of banks that colludes with our elected officials. Later in this book I discuss this travesty in more detail.

A logical question you might raise at this point is, why not start to improve our National Government where the most debt and mismanagement is rampant? A very logical question but if improving a State's financial and political status appears difficult it would be many times more difficult to begin this task at the National level. The resistance at the National level would be more difficult to overcome but suggestion on how to approach this will be offered a little further into this book.

TRANSFER MOST OF FEDERAL GOVERNMENT TO STATES

Continuing to make improvements at the State level will quickly involve the federal Government for we need to return all social programs now centered in Washington, D. C. to the States. If a democracy is to be effective as the word Democracy implies then legislation that affects people should take place as close as possible to the people being affected. At the State level more citizen can participate and the goal should be to improve Public access to legislators. Again Nebraska's unicameral Government provides an example. The objective of providing Public input into the legislative procedure is virtually impossible when government is consolidated into Washington, D. C. Let's make it a goal to offer people affected by legislation be given the opportunity to serve as the CHECKS & BALANCE and participate in the legislative procedure.

There is no question that centralizing or concentrating most of our Government programs in Washington clearly denies meaningful Public participation. This has resulted in a democracy in name only and another reason why at least one half of our population does not even bother to register to vote. Our Government is and has been a big disappointment to many U. S. residents.

So for our own wellbeing and particularly for our children and those beyond let's decide to start improving Government at the State level and simultaneously decentralize much of the federal Government. Yes a few State Governments recently succeeded in transferring federal social and health programs to be administered by their State but more effort is needed to remove all of these federal programs to the State level. State costs will increase somewhat but less than leaving every program at the federal level. Converting programs that serve State residents over to State administration and financing will be easier if you have initiated a unicameral State Government. That modification will have already reduced your cost of government by more than 50%.

Reduce the Size of the Federal Government

At this point it becomes necessary to think about major changes. After achieving independence from England a group of our Founders met in Philadelphia in 1786 to prepare a Constitution for a Democracy. There was no model to follow and so our new Nation got a Government that resembles the English Parliament with two separate legislative groups we call the Representative and a Senate. The main difference was the Public in our new Nation voted to select who would be in each legislative body. Preparing the first draft of any document is a tough job and often needs additions and corrections. Over a period of more than two centuries we have added some amendments to that original Document. It would be unusual if our Constitution was now perfect and I have made some suggestions for changes later in this book. Again keep in mind the Founders had the problem of serving a widely dispersed population and with no communication system or media. The Founders chose the best solution to their governing choice that was a Representative Republic to overcome the lack of any means of communication.

Why Cling to Custom and Tradition?

But why do we govern today some 230 years later with the same system, namely giving our vote to a Representative when electronics gives us instant communication service between each other and the world. Today our population exceeds 300 million including densely populated metropolitan areas but still we cling to a pioneer system of letting someone represent us. Unfortunately our Government consists of—that might be a bit strong, but at least our Government is dominated by Special Interests. Guess who is to blame for our lousy Government!

Later in this book I discuss decentralizing our legislators in State Capitol cities. Again it was our Pioneers that selected State Capital cities for their elected officials to hold their meetings, as there was no communication system. That served the Pioneers well but for probably the last century this concentrating elected officials in Capitol cities is equivalent to providing a "den" for elected officials and special interests to Buy and Sell votes!

How can we correct a badly deteriorated political system? Electing a person or two or even dozens that claim they will Change Government just does not work. Politicians have a fitting expression that states, "Reformers are Morning Glories" meaning the established "old guard" soon cause reformers to wilt like a Morning Glory or the reformers are set aside where they are ineffective. Our National Government is probably best described as a cancer that cannot be cured except to abandon and start over. Drastic? Yes, but look at the record—given time all Government programs become disasters! Let's face it—we are "over governed" and Congress for decades is a superfluous appendage beyond control by the voters. For a decade or more our electronic system can give the Public the chance to provide the CHECKS & BALANCE our Founders knew was essential. That improvement is waiting for the Public to become a participant, to step forward and become the balance wheel in a real Democracy.

An Improved Government is Waiting

We the people have continually ignored the Founder's advice to keep federal Government small. The Founders knew what would happen and now we know they were right but how do we change it? We also ignored the Founder's advice to avoid foreign entanglements and our record on avoiding this advice has too often embroiled us in foreign Wars. When elected officials swear allegiance to support our Constitution they are required to protect our boundaries but we allow them to adopt the foreign policy of an Empire even though history shows nations that have gone the route of an Empire have all failed and also faced bankruptcy.

It would be interesting to compare our State Department with a comparable agency in other developed nation. Between our State and Administration Departments we keep numerous Government employees constantly in the air purportedly to advise other nations. What do we have to brag about? We have the largest Public debt of any developed nation, based

To Garry and Susan:

Since your activities are somewhat limited I'm taking the chance you might read, or at least look over what contrarians are offering, at least the one living a couple doors from you. I think it safe to say many people are dissatisfied with our government, and it is also safe to predict no elected official is about to vote themselves out of office.

So, how can change ever occur? Guess it's up to the public and so far there doesn't seem to be any movement in that direction.

Hope this helps a bit to compensate for your restricted activities.

carlton

on our population we have more people in prison than other developed nations, and we have a greater drug problem to name just a few conditions most responsible nations have avoided.

For Your Consideration

Many people have given thought about what can be done to change what happens in Washington and our imbedded Congress. And for decades it has been recognized that concentrating elected officials into Washington provides a Den where elected officials can be enticed and bought by special interests that surround them. We are told the number of lobbyist is five to six times larger than the total members of Congress. Is it just a coincidence that most members of Congress are wealthy?

The same problem exists in concentrating State legislators into State Capitol cities except the financial numbers are smaller. It is easy to understand why early 20th century journalist H. L. Mencken described, "Every election is an auction of stolen goods." There is no need to elaborate on the power structure that has controlled our Nation for several decades. The Public knows our governing system is broken and it is time for some REAL change if we have the desire to make this happen!

Mark Twain observed, "It could probably be shown by facts and figures that there is no distinctly American criminal class except Congress."

Congress in particular but also in State legislatures the attitude of elected officials is that taxes collected from the Public belongs to the elected officials to use as they see fit, including outright stealing. There is no clearer case of stealing Public funds than "Earmarks" taken and even boasted as an achievement by members of Congress. Consider the stealth of Social Security funds for decades by Congress to deceive the Public on the full amount of the Public debt. Public taxes fund Social Security annually during each person's working years. And your Congress and mine annually "lifted" really stole from that fund for decades and now that the fund needs to be replaced Congress considers reducing the rate of reimbursement to the Public. There is no clearer description of Congress than, "Given time all programs established by Government become disasters!" We would benefit from a lot less Government and this book offers suggestions to achieve that.

Another disaster caused by Government—Fannie May and Freddie Mac the companion insurer of home loans was considered for years as semi-government supported. When it became apparent these two insuring agencies were financial disasters U. S. Treasurer Timothy Geithner, a former head of the New York office of the Federal Reserve, declared unilaterally in 2010 these two defunct home loan agencies would be totally Publicly owned and become the responsibility of the taxpayer! What ever happened to the alleged private sector support in this insurance coverage? Government quickly becomes the "fall guy" when the right businesses need help!

Mismanagement that often includes dishonesty has zero chance of correcting itself. Electing a few candidates that pledge to eradicate all that is wrong in Congress has never worked. The "establishment" that exists in all legislative bodies prevents newcomers and particularly alleged reformers from ever getting a start in a legislative body. In private industry an outsider can often turn a company around. That possibility does not exist in government.

A Time Tested Solution

So how can the Public gain control of their Government? This book began with emphasis on the importance of adopting unicameral government in your State. This change is essential to reduce the power of Party politics that successfully employed the technique of DIVIDE and CONQUER with the ultimately result being Grid Lock. Until enough States adopt a unicameral Government there is little hope of moving forward to correct the waste and autocratic rule by a Congress that is virtually a dominant "Fourth Estate". Of course every two to four years elected officials appear and with tongue in cheek state they are our servants. After election its back to normal with elected officials becoming the master and the Public becomes THEIR servants! Until the Public is ready to reduce the strangle hold of Congress there is little hope for what started some 230 years ago with the intention and hope the new Nation would become a beacon to the World and represent the benefits of freedom and democracy.

As previously stated a real democracy requires the people affected by proposed legislation be provided the opportunity to make an input into that legislation. That cannot happen by enlarging the National Government in Washington, D. C. The Nebraska unicameral is an example of providing the people affected by proposed legislation an opportunity to participate in the final draft of that legislation. That is BASIC and we do not come close to having Government of, for and by the people! Making laws, called Legislation, needs to be a deliberate procedure with time given for public participation, the input by people.

When enough States are prepared to take on leadership it will be time for PHILADELPHIA II, an open session to revise and update our Constitution for serving the 21st century! The World's first Constitution was drafted in 1786 in Philadelphia but it did not anticipate the partisan Party system that has evolved with the power to DIVIDE and CONQUER would deny citizen participation in Government. The Founders did not fully understand the long-range changes that would be needed for people in a real Democracy—a form of government that never existed before but in later years was adopted by Switzerland where it has been successful for more than a century.

An issue for PHILADELPHIA II is whether to abandon the present form of Congress as well as the Office of President. In 1786 George Washington could have been installed as King but contributed greatly to the new Democracy by rejecting those thoughts. Today our elected Presidents act as a King and along with a Congress equally as aggressive and an out-of-touch Government is a condition that has existed for several decades is endangering our solvency.

Problems Facing Philadelpia II

Mistakenly I'm sure the Founders put an obstacle in front of the Public by requiring approval of elected officials, our Congress to change the Constitution. If we have a real democracy the power of the people should not be restricted by some vested interest like Congress or even the Supreme Court. I mention the Court because of the action it took in the 2000 election shows it as a partisan Court. We have allowed partisan politics to determine the Supreme Court. There was ample evidence in the 2000 Florida election of mismanagement but our Supreme Court had no problem with determining our next President.

Since the political party in control of the White House influences appointments to our Supreme Court there is real doubt the politically influenced Court would allow the People to make the revisions needed in the Constitution for the 21st century. We can try but may find voters will need to continue their determination into enough elections to achieve their objective. Perfecting a Democracy is not an easy job as there are always vested interests satisfied with the status quo. On the subject of Supreme Court appointments a body consisting of heads of Department of Law in our Colleges and Universities would be better qualified to recommend appointments to the Supreme Court.

Due to years of neglect in caring for our Democracy we are saddled with an extremely expensive Congress that for several decades amounts to an unnecessary appendage that permits the power of special interest to influence government. For example Earmarks is a cunning method for Congress to steal public funds and is just one example of the belief by Congress that Public tax revenues belong to them. And as has been stated many times, all Government programs become a disaster due to inadequate administration of Government programs and continuing lack of enforcement.

The performance of Congress compares to a Police Department; it takes action after the event has taken place. The main difference between the two is Congress then holds months of costly hearings that result in no action taken other than possibly amending a law or Act that from its beginning was not properly staffed or supervised. In short Congress is an expensive waste of tens of billions of dollar and should be eliminated.

An Alternative to Congress

As individual States prepare amendments to State Constitutions to adopt the unicameral legislature each State Governor should be designated as a Representative to a new FEDERAL ASSEMBLY to replace the present Congress. That new body of 50 State Governors would meet once a month or when called by a majority of their members. Acting as Representatives in the new FEDERAL ASSEMBLY the Governors would appoint a Chief Executive of Office, the CEO that would replace the Office of President. This new CEO would serve at the pleasure of the Governors. This replacement would eliminate partisan elected Presidents and the expenditure of many billions of campaign contributions from special interest that we all know contribute in the expectation of special favors throughout the President's term of office.

These changes in the structure and organization of our State and Federal Governments will achieve putting all legislation within reach of the Public to have input into their Government. And each State that adopts a unicameral

Government would be expected to include sufficient locations around their State where State citizen can participate and provide the Checks and Balance on their State's Government. Our Nation's Founders knew this was necessary for a real Democracy but the logistics of a Pioneer society when transferred to our developed country gave special interest control. But now there is no excuse for the Public allowing this abuse to continue for over 230 years. So let's correct these abuses and make the 21st century into the Government our Founders intended!

I believe the best way to start this improvement in each State Government is to adopt a unicameral Government. In updating your State Constitution make your Governor also a Representative of a new National Assembly and this will put citizen participation closer to the voting public than has ever existed before. Fifty State Governors will comprise the decision making body of a new National Assembly that replaces the stumbling block that has prevented real democracy from ever working.

Cost Reduction Continued

We have only started in listing the costs that can be reduced in Government. By using the financing planned by the Founders but never implemented I will explain how there should be no Government debt that serves as a subterfuge for the Federal Reserve to extract a huge income off the Public on interest collected on bonded debt. All that is needed to correct this abuse to the Public is to implement the authority provided in Article 1 Section 8 of the Constitution. Lincoln was the first President to use this provision to finance the Civil War. Today any U. S. Treasury Secretary has the power to issue interest free loans to any governing entity with taxing power. This means every State, County, municipality, school district, or any special district that can levy a tax is eligible for an interest-free loan. The residents of each taxing unit should decide the amount and time needed to repay the interest free loan to the U. S. Treasurer. The taxing entity that borrows these funds should obtain the consent of its governed, meaning those affected by this tax. In this procedure the U. S. Government would have no debts, just accounts receivable due from taxing entities in the U. S. The

U. S. Government could also borrow in the same way and commit itself to repay by establishing a federal tax or use fees collected by the U. S. Government in the amount to re-pay the loan.

Imagine making Community Improvements with no interest on the cost of those improvements! Traditionally capital improvements required a bond issue and the interest on the bond issue amounted to about two thirds the total cost. The capital improvement amounted to about one third of the cost. We may think we have a democracy but our financial system is a continuation of Old Europe with the Rothschilds, now the Federal Reserve in the U. S., in charge and collecting the major cost of every improvement and investment. In short—the whole country works for the banking syndicate! The Public can change that any time they get tired of being a mere Serf to a privately owned financial system. The residents of any community can have WHATEVER THEY WANT OR A WILLING TO PAY FOR!

DEFINING REAL WEALTH

Another misconception we have is that banks create wealth—NOT TRUE. Banks live off the debt of others and banks as well as governments are parasites and that is a major reason why our Government, State and federal should be kept small. The Founders recognized this and advised us but as humans have a tendency to think someone else should support them—the basis of socialism, we opted for a system that does not work well. Real wealth is created when individuals create something of value, something others are willing to buy. The accumulated wealth of a Nation is part of THE PUBLIC DOMAIN and it should be available for the Public to use without being charged to use THEIR OWN MONEY. We need to recognize this when so much of our economy is for War and War related goods. All of this is for goods that are wasted, destroyed, and individuals injured that require medical care that consumes wealth and adds debt that banks like for they collect the loans and interest on Government borrowing.

Why isn't this basic economics taught in our schools? It is largely because a sector known as the Industrial/Military complex gets fabulous rich by destroying a Nation's wealth. Much of our Nation's thinking needs correcting. Debt does not make us rich as we are beginning to realize.

MOVE STATE LEGISLATURES OUT OF STATE CAPITALS

Adopting unicameral legislatures is only the beginning of possible costs reductions. For instance, why do all State legislatures meet in State capitol cities? A typical reply to this and other questions about government is usually, "Because we have always done it that way." The real reason of course is the Pioneers had no media, no way to communicate and they decided on what was best in their situation. Assembling elected representatives in a capitol city was often the best suited for providing lodging and eating. The real question is why has this archaic practice continued for over two centuries when for decades we have had vocal and visual communication and now even instant communications via electronics. As you recognize it is nearly impossible for Government to get out of a rut and to date the Public accepts Government inefficiency and the mounting cost.

A new and very important improvement would be to relocate elected State legislators to offices in their voting district as this would give residents of each voting district access to their legislator on proposed legislation. Taxpayer savings would be tens of millions of dollars by eliminating legislator travel expenses, lodging, food, and by adopting the policy for mechanics legislators should supply their own tools, namely a computer, copier, etc. and receive a modest allotment for depreciation. Here is another large savings with the additional benefit of providing Public input that is essential for real democracy. Of course this change has been possible for a long time but the Public allowed Government to stagnate and the Public to complain about costs.

With State legislators located in their voting district the Public would have ready access to government expenditures and require elected officials to adopt electronic communication to keep the Public informed on the financial obligations taxpayers will ultimately have to pay. A few minuets a week would keep the Public advised on our finances and the presence of each State legislature in an office in their voting district will greatly improve Government performance.

Changing Old Customs

Cost reduction could also occur in operating the United Nations if electronics was maximized to make a physical presence at the New York U. N. headquarters unnecessary. When the U. N. was established electronic communications did not exist but neither has the full potential of electronic communication been added though it has been available for a decade or more. Why doesn't someone in government recognize the importance of cost reduction to the world particularly for poorer nations? Even more affluent nations would benefit from savings that could be directed elsewhere. By extending information about the U. N. to all member nations via electronic communications there will be a better understanding of the U. N. programs throughout each nation. The momentum to initiate this change should come from larger nations like the United States and our economy will also benefit.

All of these potential savings are lost because we do not elect leaders—only followers willing to perpetuate outmoded and costly procedures. Their excuse, "It has always been done this way!" However maintaining our outmoded status quo cannot be financially maintained!

Let's move on to another ingrained Government expenditure that is annually costing taxpayer's tens of billions of dollars. It is our Ambassador system. A bit of history shows the U. S. appointed ambassadors to a few European nations starting in 1893 though a few European posts had been raised to Embassy level in 1873. Ranking in our foreign services beginning at the lower level consist of Consul, Minister and Ambassador and all are administered by our State Department. The 1924 Rogers Act was amended in 1954 to improve the Diplomatic Corp within the State Department. Following that improvement ambassador appointments were made from the State Department's Diplomatic Corp from candidates that passed tests and received Department training. But in the last half of the 20th century our Presidents began appointing ambassador as a reward for large political donations. In earlier years an Ambassador position was considered important enough to professionalize our Foreign Service representatives but for the last half of the 20th century our politically oriented Presidents have diluted the position of Ambassador to the level of politics.

So in addition to costing taxpayers billions of dollars Presidents have installed the political "Spoils systems" into our foreign services. Currently there is no incentive for a political appointee to adopt electronic capability and possibly they even shun electronics as this could shed light on excessive costs. In the 16th and 17th centuries private companies in England financed foreign ventures like the India Company. The Netherlands (Dutch), Spain and others soon followed or copied these ventures. The financial success of the India Company along with its evolving into a private government in these foreign countries attracted the greedy English government that needed more income to fund its continuous wars. This resulted in England introducing its Ambassador system and crowded out private enterprises. So our Government followed the established funding of ambassador systems and one of the main services of our ambassadors is to provide business contacts for private enterprise.

Can the cost be distributed or shared? Rather than attempt some cost sharing formula between Government and private industry cost reduction could result if the State Department and its agencies installed electronic communication with the capability of virtually eliminating the need for the physical presence of an ambassador, Consul or Minister along with a full staff component now in place in nearly every country in the world. How much could be saved? It is difficult to pick an estimated amount but it would be on the order of billions and billions that is now spent just to continue Custom & Tradition. State Department employees located right here in the U. S. could contact any foreign company for any U. S. company all via computer capability. It is almost certain that billions of tax dollars could be saved.

HAS PROHIBITION EVER WORKED?

Few people remember the prohibition of alcoholic beverages that was in effect from 1920 to 1933. It was a total failure broken by a Public that wanted the beverage and by bootleggers like the infamous Al Capone of Chicago. The making and enjoyment of these beverages extends as far back as the human race. When the Puritans sailed to that new land of Freedom, America, their ship was stocked with alcoholic beverage. Since fermentation is a process occurring in nature religions believed it was approved by God and in addition fermented liquids were more pure than many water sources.

In Inns in early America provided these favorite beverages as well as sleeping quarters. Gradually the tavern evolved. In its earliest days the tavern was still a place where families visited and it became a center for card players. Excessive drinking was not a problem while family and gatherings of close friends were the main social activity. As this changed so did drinking habits until groups like the WCTU, the Women's

Christian Temperance Union gained enough support to pass legislation prohibiting the manufacture and distribution of alcoholic beverages. Crime increased as did bootlegging and the Public recognized prohibition was not workable.

Gambling was the next attempt by Government to regulate human behavior. It was another failure. In my experience as a City Manager Police Departments spent many hours sleuthing to find gambling parties even checking on the number of cars parked in a neighborhood as a possible tip of a "game going on". Legalizing gambling was a great relief for Police Departments and it will be an even greater relief when the War on Drugs ends and each person becomes responsible for their actions. Government just makes a mess, usually a disaster of every attempt to regulate human activities and thought.

The War on Drugs is the worst disaster in Government's attempt to police and regulate human behavior. How can Government personnel from the President, the Congress, and anyone employed or associated with this futile prohibition live with their conscience? It is our POPULATION with a bad habit that is causing the death of hundreds of government and police personnel in Mexico. We even supply the weapons for this death and destruction that is spreading across the border into the U. S. The magnitude of this government fiasco warrants taxpayers warning all U. S. Government officials to legalize and administer drugs as is done with alcohol and tobacco or there will be a Recall Election to remove from office all those responsible for continuing this immoral and deadly War on Drugs! Legalizing the drugs would immediately stop the death and destruction and save billions of taxpayer dollars.

THERE IS MORE WASTE

Let's move on to another huge challenge—our Defense Department. Anyone that could not cut a few billion dollars from the 2010 Department of Defense budget should go to the foot of the class! The 2010 DOD budget including an Overseas Contingency (whatever that is?) is $633 billion. In the past several years our Defense budget has become larger than the combined military budgets of ALL OTHER NATIONS! What are we trying to prove or are we really friendless in this world?

No sooner had WWII ended than our military system began a military preparedness policy and never stopped expanding. The logic of our Generals seemed to be if Hitler could build a huge military force with bonded debt even though Germany was destitute we could do the same. During WWII U. S. residents accumulated wealth due to rationing and fewer items to buy. By 1960 that surplus was gone and bonded debt began accumulating. In 2001 the George Bush administration introduced a new twist for financing preemptive Wars like Iraq and Afghanistan with Off-Budget bonded debt. That deception was so effective the Obama administration that campaigned on CHANGE continued the same practice even though the resulting financing bubble put domestic programs in danger beginning in 2007 and 2008. Not to worry—the out-going Bush Administration used close to a Trillion dollars of taxpayer money to "stimulate" certain Wall Street banks so the bubble could continue. The incoming Obama Administration that campaigned on CHANGE continued the same support for Wall Street banks, with rhetoric supporting giant banking institutions. As noted previously banks do not create wealth but live off the debt of others.

When WWII ended in August 1945 Europe and Russia were exhausted and even today much of Europe is very cool toward wars. The physical and financial destruction in Europe after two world wars convinced most Europeans it is important to learn to live with each other. But the U. S. attitude toward war was different. We had little physical damage from the two World Wars and our Generals preferred to prepare our Nation for the next war and found enough support among former Allies in Europe to form a military alliance as a defense to any Russian threat. Hitler gained public support for his militarism by always claiming someone as an enemy. We have found that effective also.

By1949 our military leaders had created NATO. Our military leaders are not bothered by the Physical law of, "for every action there is an equal and opposite reaction". And so in 1955 as a counterweight to NATO at their doorstep Russia formed the Warsaw Pact, a collection of nations adjacent to Russia or nearby. I'm reminded of philosopher George Santayana's expression, "Those who do not remember history are likely to repeat it". We of course have forgotten, even just ignored President George Washington advice and caution to "avoid foreign entanglements with Europe".

A military mind believes military preparedness will keep out ideas like Communism and until recently the NATO Commander was always a U. S. General. Now some 60 years later we have been able to draw NATO troops into our Wars that either we started as a preemptive strike or were ask to help as in the Balkan Wars. The military makes their presence seem essential even though many in our Country are beginning to question whether we can afford the role of an Empire. If we referred to the Constitution our leaders swear to defend and protect our Nation's boundaries but we become frightened by small nations that have no navy or any real air strength. If you have a lot of War Toys you are easily spooked!

Did we stumble into a sort of International PWA (Public Works Act created during the 1930s Depression) where our military destroys, only to be followed by the U. S. Public being committed to rebuild what was destroyed? The Marshal Plan funded billions of our taxpayer money after WWII; no memorialized name was given to smaller rebuilding projects after being involved in the Balkan Wars.

When President George W. Bush led our Nation into our first preemptive War and invaded Iraq he gathered support for this unpopular adventure by collecting a "coalition" of other countries. Information on that "coalition" was scarce but the media found our Defense Department offered Turkey 15 billion dollars to allow U. S. flights over Turkey to improve our military's entrance into Iraq. Turkey demonstrated unusual morality and courage by refusing the U. S. offer. How many other bribes were offered to collect the "coalition?" Lately more evidence shows the Bush Administration obtained undocumented information even from U. S. Departments that favored his military strike into Iraq. In the previous Persian Gulf War about a decade earlier George Bush, Sr. and field General H. Norman Schwarzkopf withdrew after forcing the Iraqi army from Kuwait based on information indicating pushing into Iraq would become a Tar Pit!

What information led us into Afghanistan? If you recall 15 of the 19 men involved in bombing the New York World Towers and the Pentagon in Washington, D. C. were Saudi citizens yet that did not gain any recognitions from the Bush Administration or the Public. After the bombing in 9/11 all U. S. air traffic was suspended for 24-hours EXCEPT the Saudis were allowed to fly and collect all of their citizens in the U. S. and return them to Saudi Arabia. Michael Moore's Documentary Fahrenheit 9/11 states the Bush family have investments in Saudi Arabia and when visiting there are guests of the Saudi Royal family.

Where does Osma Ben Laden fit into this? Our news reports he was expelled from Saudi Arabia for trying to change Saudi Government, but with 15 of the 19 involved in bombing the

U. S. it suggests there was more dissent in Saudi Arabia toward the U. S. than just Ben Laden. The Saudi Government is an outgrowth of rural tribes and continues with barbaric practices of chopping off heads and hands in what is referred to as Chop Chop Park. You and I would not want to live in Saudi Arabia because socially it is a backward nation. Saudi women are virtually prisoners of ancient custom. In addition the Saudi version of Islam is quite different but all Islam objects to foreign troops in their land. Don't we have the same attitude?

To protect the ruling Government of Saudi Arabia the U. S. has for years maintained a sizeable military presence of around 10,000 troops in Saudi Arabia to protect oil interest though our actual import of oil from the Saudis is a small part of our total oil import. But we also have a military presence in at least 100 other nations through arrangements with the non-democratic leaders in those nations. The public in those nations finds our presence objectionable, but we only ponder why much of the world dislikes the U. S. Can you find the missing piece to this puzzle? Should the invasion into Afghanistan to find Ben Laden been done by the Saudis?

Does any of this remind you of Jonathan Swifts' "Gulliver Travels" where the "little people" tied up the Giant? In our 10-year War in Afghanistan the "little people" the Al Qaeda and Taliban cannot muster an army to defeat us but they have said, "We will bankrupt you." So who is winning?

It still takes two to tango and when George Bush decided to pursue Ben Laden though this meant invading another foreign country that move brought few objections in the U. S. It has not been shown there was any evidence the Afghan nation invited Ben Laden to seek refuge in their country. It would seem we would have considered the Afghans are poor people with an inadequate government and little control over who sneaks into the nearly impenetrable mountain border with Pakistan? Did we move into Afghanistan as a favor to the Saudis or do our War Presidents enjoy the power and the wealth that transcends to the Military/Industrial complex that in the past were liberal campaign contributors?

Is There A Wake Up Call?

After years of wasteful and reckless spending our economy became warped though a common opinion was our growing debt gave us a feeling of being wealthy. We waltzed to that tune for decades and even when General Eisenhower warned us of the Industrial/Military Complex in his retirement comments as President of the U. S. his remarks drew little attention. We even let succeeding presidents finance our next wars "off budget" even though debt from wars and unfilled legislative commitments had increased the "PUBICS" debt obligation to close to 80 Trillion dollars. That amount is so far beyond belief we go blithely along—though our children and grand children will question our sanity!

Opinion polls taken by leading U. S. magazines prior to the March 2003 invasion of Iraq found 2 out of 3 residents wanted our Government to wait until the U. N. inspectors finished their work in Iraq. Only 31% approved immediate military invasion of Iraq. (From the Internet) President Bush stated early in March 2003 "the U. N. is irrelevant". On March 19, 2003 the U. S. Army invaded Iraq, historic in being our

Nation's first preemptive strike against another nation. Later we were to learn the optimistic information released to justify that War was mistaken and our own Security personnel relied on unsupported leads. Our Government responded by ridiculing other Nation's leaders for not supporting our invasion of Iraq. Perhaps you may have forgotten but our Governing leaders made fun of those that did not support our Iraq invasion like suggesting "French fries" should be re-named since France did not support us!

As the Iraq War slogged on year after year we did not "eat crow" or ever admit mistakes and we were not even embarrassed to finally ask for help from the U. N. and for European nations to help train Iraqis to take over a country we destabilized and caused the death of thousands and more millions to flee their country. Although it is disputed there was no Al Qaeda in Iraq until U. S. troops arrived and the infiltration of Al Qaeda is a spontaneous resistance that wants foreign troops to vacate Muslim countries. The natural law "For every force there is an equal and opposite force" seems to escape our foreign policy!

The Mother of All Rip-Offs

In several previous books I have written I've described the continuing financial problems as our new Nation grew and expanded. The Founders were well aware of the political and financial oppression in Old Europe and they made a special effort to correct both problems in what would be the world's first democracy. Our history books do not adequately describe the growth pains our Pioneer experienced in the absence of any form of a media and communications system. In recent years the individual biographies of early leaders like John Adams, Benjamin Franklin and Thomas Jefferson make you realize the great voids in information these leaders faced in the absence of a media. Fortunately whenever these leaders were assembled to prepare policy for the new Nation they maintained the initial objective for pursuing a Democracy dedicated to supporting individual freedom.

One costly blip that occurred and resulted in consequences that have extended to the present day was the Commonwealth of Massachusetts granting a bank charter to entrepreneur Alexander Hamilton in 1782. The Revolutionary War had not ended until 1784 but Hamilton recognized the monetary value when banks extend credit to Governments and Hamilton gambled the new Government of these pioneers would be deeply in debt and he wanted to be in position to be rewarded. It was this Old World type bank charter that plagues our economy today.

After the War ended in 1784 travel to Europe to conclude a Peace Treaty took years that extended the time to draft a new Constitution in Philadelphia to 1786. Again the wisdom gained from first-hand experience with oppression in Old Europe resulted in the Founders inserting a provision in the new Constitution, Article 1 Section 8 that would give the new Government the authority to prevent anyone gaining a monopoly on the new Nation's financial system. The lack of communications caused this grievous error, namely, the bank charter granted to Hamilton by Massachusetts opened control of banking to private control.

Hamilton's first bank failed and his application for another was being debated when the War of 1812 with England occurred and this again prevented a thorough analysis of the situation. Jefferson among others questioned issuing the new banking license but after the British burned down the start of a new Government in Washington and the overall struggle of this new Nation's Government another bank charter was issued. During Andrew Jackson's Presidency 1828-1836 Jackson was aware of the threat of the financial monopoly and in very strong words refused to renew a bank charter for the monopoly Hamilton had started. Again the lack of an adequate media to inform our leaders as well as the Public resulted in a financial problem for a new and expanding nation continued.

The new and expanding Nation needed a steady increase in the money supply and small private banks attempting to serve their communities were not capable to meet the demand. The typical local bank was started by a few individuals and often extended so much credit that bad weather and a crop failure would cause bank failures. But bank failures were different then, a few stockholders would lose money but soon new banking ventures would start up. This procedure was repeated over and over and the new Nation was continually short of money for its continuing growth.

An important financial event happened in 1861 when newly elected Abraham Lincoln needed to finance the Civil War. Banks wanted 25% interest on borrowed money. But self-educated Lincoln knew the Constitution and implemented Article 1 Section 8 that states, "Congress shall coin and regulate the currency". Lincoln's Secretary of the Treasury issued $450 million non-interest bearing Government bonds and the Congress levied a small tax to repay the bonds. As I recall the tax collect an amount representing about one-forth the amount of the bond issue whereas bank loans over the four years of War would have equaled the full amount of the bond issue.

Of course banks were livid over Lincoln's protection of the Public's tax money by critically referring to the notes as "greenbacks" and refusing to redeem the notes at full value though they carried the full faith and credit of the federal government. That War ended in 1865, Lincoln was shot shortly after beginning his second term in office and the interest free bonds were finally redeemed at full value about 1871.

The Nation's economy continued to struggle to meet the financial demand of its rapid growth that had periodic booms and busts about every four to five years. The 1907 recession got widespread attention, as it was so severe it affected the northeast States where previous financial slumps had been mild due the industrial development in that area. Complaints to Congress increased but elected officials never seemed to know the cause or the remedy for the booms and busts in the economy.

The 1907 recession drew the attention of bankers and around 1912 Senator Nelson W. Aldrich of Rhode Island who had wide interest in banking wrote the Federal Reserve Act. After some promotion and delays an amenable and compliant Congress passed the Federal Reserve Act in 1913. The 1913 Congress and most members of Congress ever since have supported giving our Nation's financial system to this privately owned banking system. The Federal Reserve Act was exceptionally generous for it granted this privately owned banking syndicate exemption from all U. S. taxes, all audits and all State and federal supervision and regulation and topped this gift by allowing the Federal

Reserve to operate as a secret society. Are we to believe we have a Democracy!

The 1913 Congress, Senator Aldrich who drafted the Federal Reserve Act, and every member of Congress since then ignored Section 19 of the U. S. Coinage Act of 1792. The new U. S. Government was establishing its own Monetary System and Section 19 of the Çoinage Act states: " . . . . anyone guilty of debasing gold and silver coins shall be put to death." At that time currency or paper money had not been established, all commerce was conducted with coins. Though it could be argued the use of currency is not applicable, it is the currency the paper money that has been debased and a Government that believes in a stable monetary system, of keeping the value of the Public's money steady and consistent from day to day and year to year would require all forms of money to remain constant. That was not the intent of the banking syndicate that established and supports the Federal Reserve System.

FLEECING THE PUBLIC

With the collusion of Congress our monetary system is the equivalent of a balloon—the Federal Reserve expands and deflates our currency at will. And when the interest rate is dropped to zero or anything below the cost of living every salary and savings is drained or vacuumed into the coffers of banks. This is done periodically to reinforce bank losses in toxic loans. In this monetary scam there is nothing backing or supporting our money except the power of Congress to tax the Public. I repeat, we do not have a Government by, for and of the people—in short our entire population works for the banks!

A Bad Stumble

From our Nation's humble start and it may have been done innocently, the granting of a bank charter to Alexander Hamilton in 1782 by the Commonwealth Massachusetts opened the door to Old Europe's financial oppression. Our Founders believed they were starting the world's first democracy to become a beacon of freedom to the world but instead we laid the ground works for Old Europe's financial and political oppression.

The Ghost of Old Europe

In Old Europe a member of the Rothschild dynasty Mayer Amschel Rothschild stated in 1790, "Let me control a nation's money and I care not who makes the laws." (From the Internet; also repeated by a later Rothschild in 1838.) Today as we witness each of our National elections it is evident the control of our money also gives control of the political system. Everything remains the same regardless of which political Party is in office, or as stated before DIVIDE AND CONQUER really works.

No current or recent member of Congress, except Representative Ron Paul of Texas has tried to change the Federal Reserve even though it collects interest on the Public's use of the Public's own money. To gain passage of the Federal Reserve Act in 1913 the Bill was promoted with these claims:

    1. It would provide full employment.
    2. It would stabilize prices.
    3. It would balance International trade and payments.

You will recognize from the above tabulation the Federal Reserve has failed to fulfill all of the initial claims used to get passage of the Act in 1913. A 1913-dollar is now worth less than five cents, $0.05 verifying the effect of inflating our money that is really a sinister tax on the Public. A sound money system would keep the same value year after year but would not provide income that banks want.

With the record noted on the most glaring abuses in our economy why do your Misrepresentatives continue to increase the power of this privately owned special interest banking system that either missed or chose to ignore its initial objectives? The Federal Reserve is now urging inflation, a tool to benefit bankers by skimming off the Public's savings and earnings. Again Congress remains silent as the Federal Reserve buys up the toxic assets of banks that will be added to the Public debt. When the Federal Reserve "monetizes" the National debt that they with the help of Congress have created what does that mean? Monetizing is part of the "MAGIC" your elected officials gave the Federal Reserve and is as authentic as "PIXIE DUST"! This thievery has been going on for nearly 100 years—isn't it about time you supported a major shake up, a change in our Government?

JFK Tried to Correct This System

Earlier in this book I mentioned President Lincoln had protected the Public's wealth represented by the Public Domain by adopting the provision in our Constitution to issue interest-free money to finance the Civil War. Unfortunately Lincoln was assassinated as he began his second term in office and no President or member of Congress since then has had the courage or intelligence to continue this practice until President John F. Kennedy applied the basic principle of sound money and issued Executive Order 11110 June 4, 1963. President Kennedy's Document 100.1.2.0 on the Internet states:

"The high office of the President has been used to foment a plot to destroy the American freedom and before I leave office I must inform the Citizens of this plot". More than $4 billion in U. S. Notes in $2, $5, and $10 denominations were brought into circulation. The $20 Notes were being printed when President Kennedy was assassinated November 22, 1963 and within five months all the new U. S. Notes issued as directed by JFK were immediately taken out of circulation. The Vested interest stepped forward since the Public would not be charged interest to on the new U. S. Notes whereas the Federal Reserve collects interest from the Public on all the other currency in circulation. You be the judge why the two Presidents that applied Article 1 Section 8 of our Constitution were assassinated. That provision permits the Public to use its own currency free of interest.

MAINTAINING FREEDOM

The purpose of this book is to explain why the lack of Public participation in what was intended to be a Government by, for and of the people was converted into a scam run by special interests. This can be CHANGED any time the Public wants to give just a little time to their Government. In every community there are people ready and willing to serve as "the Minute Men" of colonial times but there needs to be the mechanism in place for interested people to use and gain access into Government and inform others to take the necessary action. For decades we have all stood idle while our resources and even our Freedom have eroded. To CHANGE this is as easy as adopting a unicameral Government in your State and selecting convenient locations where the Public can become the CHECKS & BALANCE along with presenting Public input on each piece of legislation. Government does not belong to an isolated group of legislators in each Capitol City or a Congress whose usefulness disappeared long ago but continues enjoying Public support while enjoying the life of Royalty.

My early life began before WWII. There were no subsidies, no health plan and none of the social service agencies that have been added. An ingrained philosophy made each person responsible for his or her actions. Government was not considered responsible for providing everyone a job. I recall the FDR (Roosevelt) era trying to reverse that prior philosophy by creating Government debt (a joy to banks and the Federal Reserve) but regardless of FDR's pump priming the Depression lingered for 10 years when WWII rescued FDR. As far as we know the human species is the only species believing someone else should provide their support.

There is a universal excuse for all action in Government, it is, "We have always done it that way." Hence the reason George W. Bush's Administration that was followed by the Obama Administration used the same antidote for a recession, namely shovel Public money into Government programs. There was one difference in FDR's programs—his were directed mostly toward local Work Programs. Bush and Obama prefer to help those at the top—the Wall Street tycoons. Modern Presidents prefer helping those at the Top and rely on "Trickle Down" doing the rest. It is doubtful this theory is in any books on Economics but Presidents as well as most elected officials are more comfortable with people they find higher up—in rarified air. Only during campaigns is the rhetoric slanted to what the Public longs to hear. Unfortunately our Nation's financial problem will not be solved with the "rhetoric from on high" but for quite some time now the stimulus of taxpayer money is proving an elixir for banks!

In Summary

Unfortunately it appears the future may be a long and possibly painful experience as many nations concentrate on rescuing themselves from enormous Public and Private debts and try to avoid a financial collapse. The U. S. as a new nation in 1789 came onto center stage as the World's first real Democracy. Expectations were high and immigration surged for decades. In today's world the longing for Freedom and Democracy still persists but no nation has copied exactly our governing structure. This book's message addresses the need to simplify our Governing structure to give the Public the opportunity to participate in the legislative process. The Public should and will provide the best CHECKS & BALANCE and re-establish the Founders dream of making this New Nation a beacon to the WORLD of FREEDOM and DEMOCRACY. It is not too late as a huge part of the World is still searching for that wonder, namely Freedom!

Mr. Laird is a graduate of the School Of Engineering, University of Wisconsin. He was employed as an engineer for manufacturing companies followed by about 30 years serving as a City Manager for six municipalities, then editor of the American City magazine, a consultant for a New Town, a consultant on a water system for Addis Ababa, Ethiopia and Finance Director for the Commercial Fisheries Division in Alaska's Department of Fish And Game. In 1952 and 1954 was an unsuccessful candidate for the U. S. House of Representatives from the then existing Fourth Congressional District of Nebraska.

Edwards Brothers Malloy
Thorofare, NJ USA
May 10, 2012